THIS BOOQ IS DEDICATED TO THOSE WITH A CREATIVE SOUL WHO SEEK OUT ADVENTURE AND DREAM OF A BRIGHT FUTURE.

ISBN 978-0-9936428-2-1

CHOCOLATESOOPSTUDIO.COM

HELLO!!!

THANK YOU FOR PURCHASING THIS BOOK! ROBOTS ARE A TOPIC OF ENDLESS FASCINATION FOR ME. THEY'RE THE ONLY ELEMENT OF SCI-FI, HORROR AND FANTASY GENRES THAT HAS AND WILL EVER STEP OUT OF THE REALM OF FICTION AND INTO THE WORLD OF FACT. I SEE THEM AS A PERFECT MIRROR OF HUMANS. AFTER COMING INTO THE WORLD, THEY BEGIN THE DAUNTING TASK OF LEARNING ABOUT EVERYTHING AROUND THEM. FINE TUNING THEMSELVES AS THEY ADAPT TO THEIR ENVIRONMENT. ALL IN PURSUIT OF BECOMING BETTER.

THROUGHOUT MY CHILDHOOD AND ADULT LIFE, DRAWING HAS BEEN THE ONE THING THAT HAS ALLOWED ME TO FOCUS THE CHAOTIC SUPER POWER OF HAVING ADHD. DRAWING HAS ALWAYS BEEN A RELAXING WAY TO LOSE MYSELF IN THE CREATIVE PROCESS. CREATING THIS BOOK HAS BEEN A LOT OF FUN AND CHALLENGING. MY GOAL WAS TO CAPTURE A MOMENT IN EACH IMAGE AND LEAVE IT TO YOU TO IMAGINE WHAT HAPPENED JUST BEFORE OR WHAT HAPPENS NEXT IN THE STORY. HAVE FUN EXPLORING THE 32 IMAGES AS YOU BRING THEM TO LIFE WITH COLOUR. SO GET CRAZY AND BRING YOUR FLAVOUR TO EACH PICTURE. REMEMBER, THE MOST IMPORTANT THING IS TO JUST HAVE FUN WITH IT!

IF YOU ENJOY THIS THE ART AND SUBJECT MATTER OF THIS BOOK, COME OVER AND FIND ME ON INSTAGRAM FOLLOW @CHOCOLATESOOP AND SAY HELLO! #ROBOTCOLOURINGBOOQ

LET'S JUMP IN!!!

BUILD IT TOGETHER »

GO ON A QUEST »

BE PLAYFUL »

CHALLENGE YOURSELF »

UNLOCK THE SECRET LEVEL »

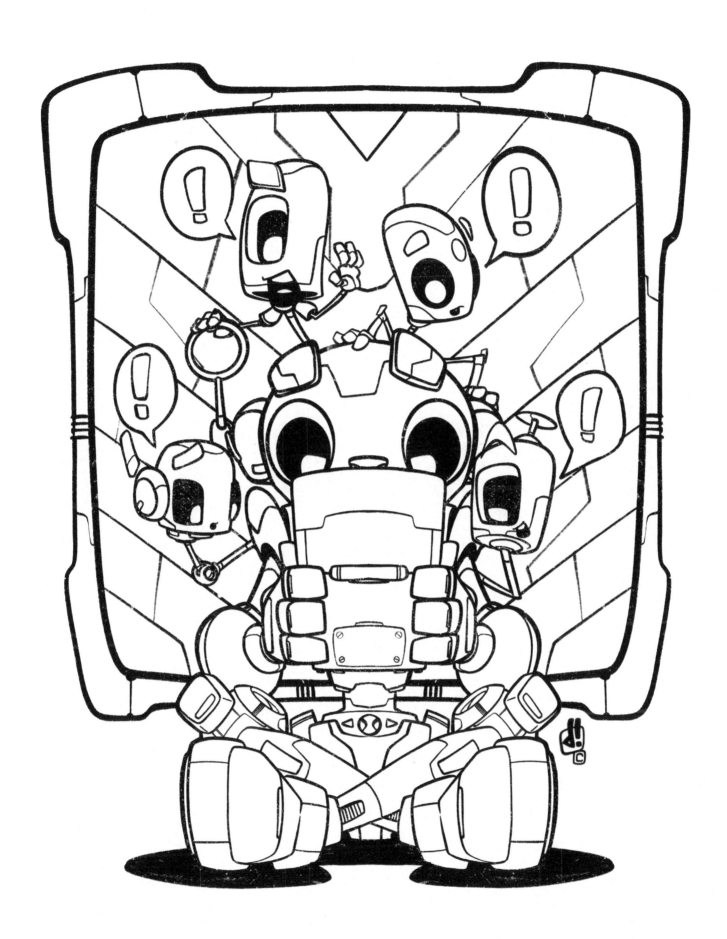

ARCADE DELIGHTS »

RIDE'EM HIGH »

TO THE RESCUE »

TEAMWORK MAKES THE DREAM WORK! »

SURPRISE GREETINGS »

HAVE A PARADE »

CELEBRATE LIFE »

EXPLORE THE WONDERS OF THE EARTH »

...AND THE DEEP BLUE SEA »

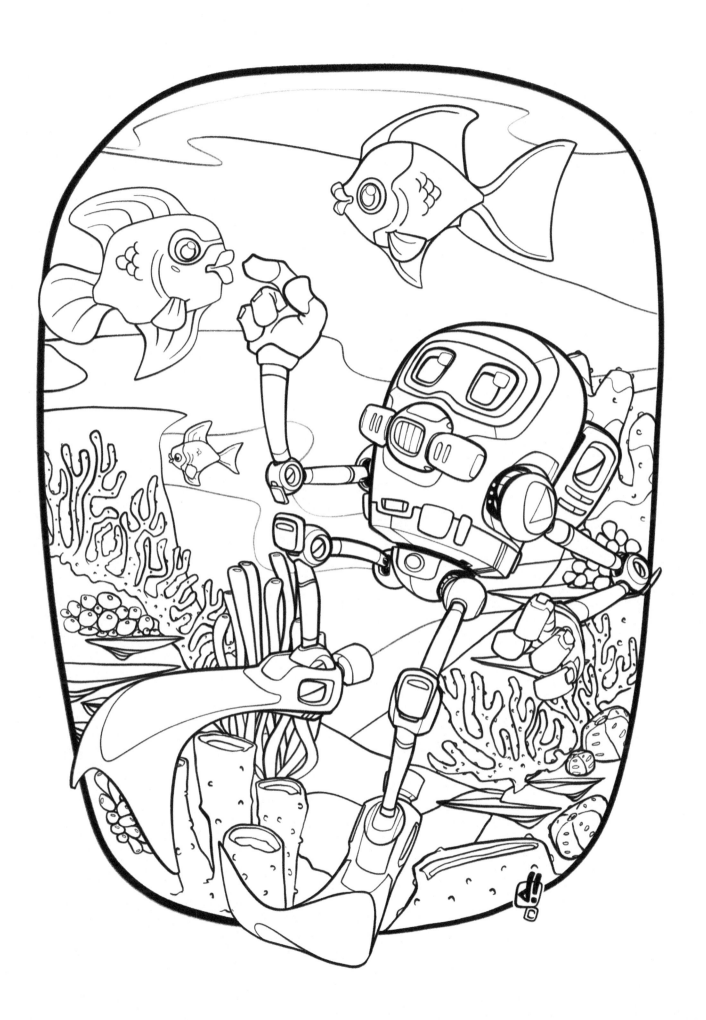

LET THE WINDS CARRY YOU »

DISCOVER A HIDDEN GARDEN »

CAPTURE THE MOMENT »

CONNECT WITH NATURE »

STEP THROUGH NEW DOORWAYS »

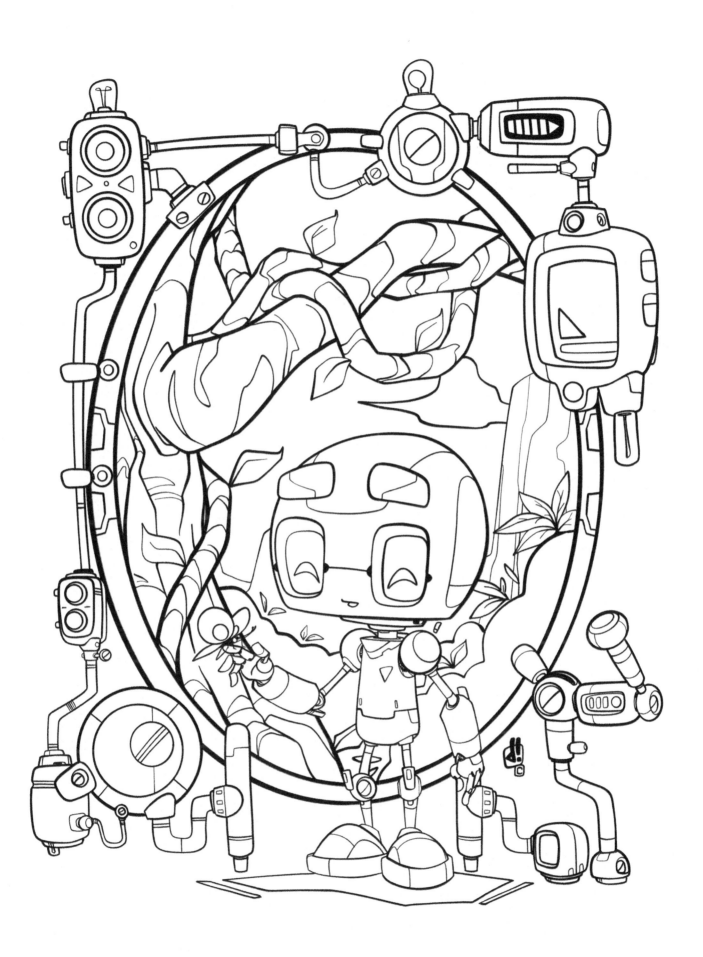

CREATE A NEW FORMULA >>

DREAM OF THE STARS »

EXPLORE NEW WORLDS »

REFRESH YOURSELF »

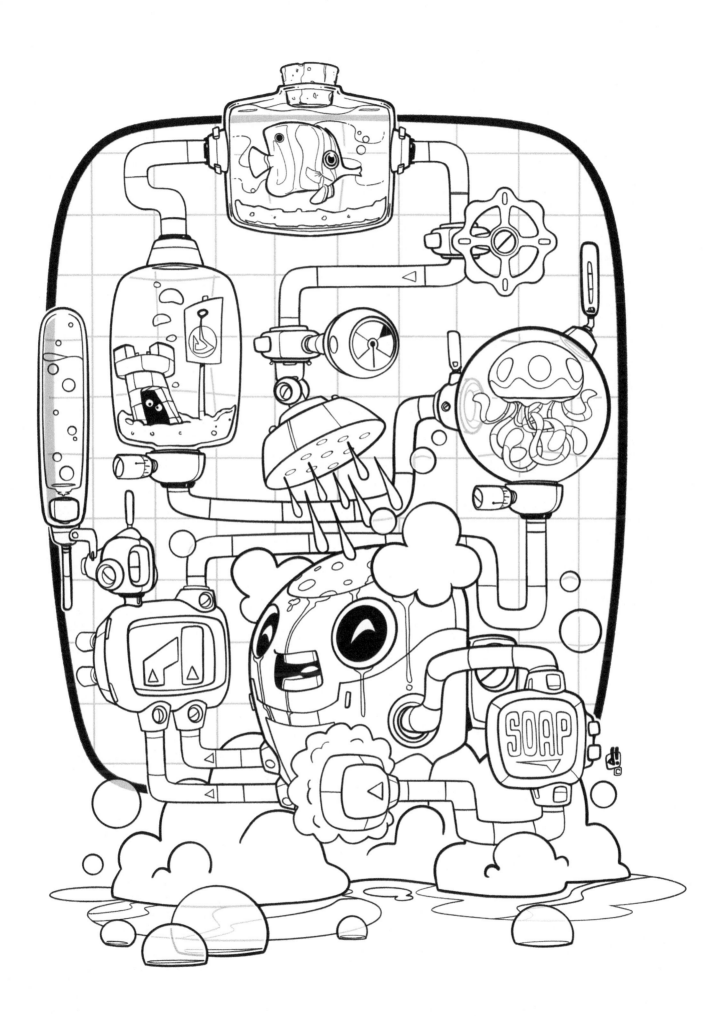

SOME THINGS DON'T GO AS PLANNED »

EXPECT THE UNEXPECTED »

EMBRACE THE DAY! »

SHARE SOME TIME TOGETHER »

SHOW YOUR IMAGINATION »

SEE YOU OUT THERE!!!

Made in United States
North Haven, CT
17 April 2022